The Joy Factor

The Joy Factor

Jep Hostetler

Herald Press
Scottdale, Pennsylvania
Waterloo, Ontario

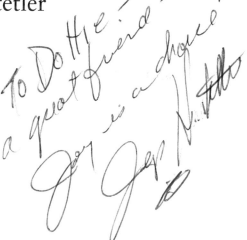

To Dottie:
a great friend
Joy is a choice.
Jep H...tler

Library of Congress Cataloging-in-Publication Data

Hostetler, Jeptha R.
  The joy factor / Jep Hostetler.
  p. cm.
  Includes index.
  ISBN-13: 978-0-8361-9364-0 (pbk. : alk. paper)
  1. Joy—Religious aspects—Christianity. 2. Happiness—Religious aspects—
Christianity. 3. Christian life—Humor. 4. Wit and humor—Religious aspects—
Christianity. 5. Hostetler, Jeptha R. I. Title.
  BV4647.J68H67 2007
  248.4—dc22
                                          2006036468

THE JOY FACTOR
Copyright © 2007 by Herald Press, Scottdale, Pa. 15683
   Published simultaneously in Canada by Herald Press,
   Waterloo, Ont. N2L 6H7. All rights reserved
Library of Congress Catalog Card Number: 2006036468
International Standard Book Number: 978-0-8361-9364-0
Printed in the United States of America
Book design by Sandra Johnson
Cover by Sans Serif
Cover art by William C. Jarvis

12 11 10 09 08 07   10 9 8 7 6 5 4 3 2 1

To order or request information, please call 1-800-245-7894, or visit
www.heraldpress.com.

Dedication

*To my mother, Luella Vivian Lehman Hostetler,
who exemplified, embodied, and fostered joy.*

Contents

Appendixes

Foreword

As a high school teacher, I often use humor to defuse student stress. On a recent Mennonite history test, for example, I asked, "When was the February 24, 1527, Schleitheim Confession written?" I enjoyed the various expressions on my students' faces as they tried to figure out whether this was a trick question or a gift. By the time my young scholars realized the latter, there was a more light-hearted atmosphere in the room. Just prior to handing out the test, I had said, "Remember, some day you will look back on all of this and laugh."

By placing the "joke question" at the beginning of the test, I had unwittingly introduced one of Jep Hostetler's important principles: "Why can't 'some day' be today?"

The Joy Factor is a good-natured and thoughtful reflection on the importance of approaching life with a positive attitude, an upbeat heart, and a can-do spirit. Jep Hostetler encourages us to tap into joy's deep springs, especially when happiness is nowhere to be found.

Early on, he draws an instructive distinction between the two: "Happiness is circumstantial, temporal, fleeting. Happiness involves the congruence of good things in our lives: health, shelter, food, good relationships, success, and children who behave. Joy is a much deeper sense of internal celebration, stability, buoyancy, and steadiness. Joy is spiritual depth and self-awareness. Joy is like a deep, wide, slow-moving river. You can be on a river of joy in a boat full of sorrow."

Jep invites us to journey with him on a meandering trip down joy's river, and he promises us some fun along the way. You'll likely enjoy a belly laugh or two, wipe away a tear, take encouragement from Hostetler's homespun stories, and come to love their compassionate main characters.

Jep reminds us that life is a gift, a sacred experience. It is usually difficult, definitely short, often funny, and always a spiritual journey.

I was particularly moved by the author's description of the note he received from his mother as he prepared to run a marathon to celebrate his sixty-fifth birthday. She sent twenty-six scripture verses—one for each letter of the alphabet—for him to memorize while he trained for the race. Only later did she find out that a marathon is twenty-six miles long. This story reminded me that joy and encouragement connect us in profound ways as we travel life's road together.

I hope you enjoy this book as much as I did. And I pray that we all remember to live out its healing message, captured beautifully in a familiar biblical aphorism: "A merry heart doeth good, like a medicine" (Proverbs 17:22).

Tim Wiebe, author, *The Timsights Treasury*
Gretna, Manitoba, March 2007

Introduction

All who would win joy must share it;

happiness was born a twin. —Lord Byron

My father was certain the summer of 1939 was one of the hottest on record in Ohio. Mother *knew* it was, as she suffered through delivering her fifth child in a non-air-conditioned bedroom in Orrville, with her sister serving as midwife.

Mother really wanted another girl. Boys were all right, but she already had plenty of them. Instead she got me, Jeptha, a six-pound, four-ounce "blue baby" boy. After considerable sputtering, coughing, and screaming, the valve between the chambers of my upper heart finally closed, and my color became normal.

Knowing Mom's desire for a baby girl, Doc Grady offered her five hundred dollars if she would give me up for adoption; he knew a family willing to buy a baby boy. Fortunately, for me, this reinvigorated the mothering instinct, and I became a Hostetler. I can't prove it, but this bumpy entrance into the world may be why I became someone known for good humor.

Few people in the United States are named Jeptha. But it's a common name in my family, handed down from my grandfather and my great-grandfather before him. Mother shortened it to Jeppy—as she shortened the names of my closest siblings to Ronnie, Danny, and Jaynie.

We four were, in effect, the second family of Emerson and Luella Hostetler. Our three older siblings—David, Anne, and John—were their "first." None of those three got their names shortened. So there we were, two in one, seven in all. Let the joy begin!

It wasn't as though our household was filled with constant joy. It was just that Mother's gentleness and eternal optimism combined with Dad's good humor and a supportive church network gave us children a relatively joyful environment in which to grow up.

We were not dirt poor. But we were certainly not in the company of the affluent. There were chores to be done, cows to be milked, wood to be brought in, floors to be mopped, crops to be planted, dishes to be washed, baths to be taken (once a week) and, of course, everything to be done all over again. Every summer we went barefoot when the temperature reached seventy degrees (Fahrenheit). At eighty degrees, we could go swimming—but not on Sundays. Mom would simply not allow it.

Our house was filled with optimism and a can-do attitude. It was common knowledge in the community that Hokey (as my father was called) was prone to patch things together, slap a coat of paint on the final product, then stand back and admire his work. It was not in his nature to use new material for an entire job. For example, he framed our new home with oak two-by-fours from a house he had torn down. While this wasn't all bad—some of the older wood was better than newer white pine—his completed jobs were not always up to Mother's—and other folks'—standards.

This doesn't mean we had fun all the time. It is not fun milking cows by hand at six a.m. when it's four degrees outside. Cutting wood with snow flying and wind howling is not a hearthside moment. Helping Dad clean the building after school was a bit embarrassing, since my peers knew my father was the janitor. Nonetheless, optimism prevailed.

But with five boys and two girls, together with numerous cousins and neighborhood children, it was easy to have fun playing together. We made up our own softball teams. We explored ponds, haymows, and open fields on our ninety acres. There was always a dog or two and at least six outdoor cats. In addition, we had large animals, including cows, pigs, and a horse named Jeannie. My brothers put me on Jeannie bareback and smacked her rump. The bumpy, frightening ride across the field that resulted is forever etched on my brain. I despised that horse.

Our family went to church at least three times a week: Sunday morning, Sunday evening, and midweek prayer meeting. I loved church picnics and potlucks; they were the only times I could eat deviled eggs. Church and family were intertwined. Our church friends were family friends, and our social circles were almost exclusively church related.

This culture became a safe place for me to try my hand at doing magic, playing piano or trombone, presenting one-person plays or shows. In other words, I was generally performing for anyone who would listen. Perhaps the performance mode was a result of being from a large family; it gave me a way to get attention.

Nearly every Sunday, especially in the summer, we spent the afternoon visiting both sets of grandparents. As a teenager, I grumbled about having to go visit relatives every Sunday. I wanted to go swimming. Dad told me that someday I would look back on those Sunday afternoons with joy and fondness. Turns out he was right.

Mom would play hymns now and then on the old upright piano, which I doubt was ever tuned. She thought I had a nice voice. Moms are like that. She encouraged me to attempt solos, and we even sang a duet together at our church. It was our first and last duet.

Then there was the time I found myself in front of all those people, singing an old, familiar children's song, "I have a joy, joy, joy, joy, down in my heart." I suppose it was passable. Our church friends *ooohhhed* and *aaaahhed* as they would over any performance by a five-year-old. Trouble is, I struggled through that solo. As I became more and more frightened, I kept singing, "I have a joy, joy, joy . . . " with the tears sneaking down my cheeks.

That experience was certainly not joy!
But what is joy?

In our culture today, we see lots of references to joy: *The Joy of Cooking, The Joy of Sex, The Joy of Pi,* and *The Joy of Farming.* Unfortunately, joy is usually equated with happiness. But they're not the same. Happiness is circumstantial, temporal, fleeting. Happiness involves the congruence of good things in our lives: health, shelter, food, good relationships, success, and children who behave.

Joy is a much deeper sense of internal celebration, stability, buoyancy, and steadiness. Joy is spiritual depth and self-awareness. Joy is like a deep, wide, slow-moving, sparkling river. You can be on a river of joy in a boat full of sorrow.

For Christians, joy is associated with God. "The joy of the Lord is my strength," we sing. Or "Joy to the world," and "Joy is flowing like a river." Even so, it's difficult to come to agreement on how to define *joy.* We might agree that joy is related to being true to one's self-understanding and to the beauty of searching for and discovering truth.

For the past twenty years, it has been my privilege to speak on the subject of joy. Afterward, as I listen to people from all walks of life talk about their joy, I've become convinced that joy is a choice one makes. Joy is obtainable.

For me, joy is the quiet peace of a life well lived, a mind well fed, and a celebration of the human spirit, regardless of circumstances.

Joy is like a deep, steady river—slowly moving, bubbly in spots, churning at times, quiet, vibrant.

Anne Sexton wrote, "The joy that isn't shared, I've heard, dies young." For Mother Teresa, joy was "the infallible evidence of the presence of God."

In this book, *The Joy Factor*, I offer some of what I've learned as I've traveled throughout the world, talking with many people about joy. What does it mean to be a person of joy?

We'll look first at the joyful life. What are the attitudes that make living a celebration? I've discovered six:

1. Life is a gift.
2. Life is sacred.
3. Life is difficult.
4. Life is short.
5. Life is funny.
6. Life is a spiritual journey.

In a final section, we'll consider how to become people of joy. Here I introduce the subject of humor, which many have asked me to talk and write about. We'll investigate how we become the people we are with the attitudes we have toward life and also look for ways we can deliberately choose and nurture joy in our daily living.

All of us can be persons of joy. It's a matter of choice, perspective, attitude, and devotion. May what follows help you cultivate joy.

Part I

Attitudes of Joy

— 1 —

Life Is a Gift

The mere sense of living is joy enough.

—Emily Dickinson

My father was an exuberant man. He loved life, and he loved living it to the fullest. Emerson Hostetler had a jack-of-all-trades reputation in our community. That reputation was the result of his being a barber, house painter, janitor, bus driver, landlord, entrepreneur (though never very successful), and farmer.

He was a rather round mound of sound. Though basically a healthy man, Dad did carry more weight on his five-foot-eight-inch frame than was good for him. "Large bones," he would explain—and then laugh.

When Dad laughed, he would intertwine his fingers as he rested his hands on his chest, and his arms would flap a bit. He enjoyed laughter, a good joke, magical entertainment, singing, and practical jokes. These all brought him the friendship of a wide variety of folks.

Dad was easy to spot in a crowd. He stuck out with his bib overalls and steel-toed, high-top, genuine leather shoes (water-proofed by periodic treatment with Neatsfoot oil). He had gray hair for most of his life.

He also had curious habits. Whenever he wanted to justify a major purchase, he would simply say, "Cigarette money." Not that he smoked, but since he didn't, why not use the money he saved for whatever it was he wanted.

Dad was a talker and a storyteller. He had rough edges. That meant people either enjoyed being around him or were a bit embarrassed by his rather crude approach to life. But he was full of vigor, eager to work, quick to delegate, and, above all, filled with compassion. That was why he often had to buy new tools to replace the ones that occasionally seemed to "walk" off our property.

All this changed dramatically one autumn. Dad was seventy-two, out painting a barn from a small stepladder, when he realized something was wrong with his legs. They tingled and then went numb. I'm not sure how he made it home. But when he got there, he went to bed, and within three days he was completely paralyzed from his neck down to his toes. How could this be? One day he was a healthy man painting a barn; three days later he was motionless except for his head.

Dad was diagnosed with Guillain-Barré Syndrome (GBS), a disease of the nerves often leading to paralysis. Although it can be life threatening, most people recover with few lasting problems. Over time, the nerves heal and begin to work more-or-less properly.

So Dad started the long road to recovery. His family was concerned about him, wondering whether or not he had the spunk to fight for recovery. After all, he had had a good life, he had worked hard, and he had a wife and seven grown children and their spouses who cared about him—to say nothing about a host of grandchildren who enjoyed his antics. There was a possibility that Dad would give up and allow the disease to win.

Much to our wonder and delight, Dad decided to fight! With the aid of physical therapists and a persistent spirit—not to mention a wife who attended to him day and night—Dad began to recover. It was slow at first, taking months for his fingers to begin to move and even more months for his wrists and arms to begin functioning. Once his arms gained some strength, he was ready for the next step.

The family put a pulley in the bedroom ceiling directly over Dad's feet. We made a large canvas and metal sling that we attached to a rope and threaded it through the pulley with the loose end within Dad's grasp. It was not a pretty contraption! But it served the purpose. Dad was able to use a long-handled garden hoe to hook one foot at a time and put it inside the sling. Then with both legs in the sling, he used the rope to raise and lower his legs. This he did several times a day.

Within two years Dad was able to walk again. True, he used two canes and some braces on his shoes, but he could walk! At seventy-five, he could drive a car again—though he did have difficulty getting it to stop at the right spot. He lived to be eighty-four.

In a sense, Dad had two lives: one before GBS, one afterward. What a gift!

People of joy have this uncanny ability to understand that life is the ultimate gift. It's not something we earn, pay for, or create. It is simply there, day by day, for us to enjoy. Even when we do not get another chance like Dad did, we can still celebrate the gift of life, at this moment, at this time.

There are many ways to celebrate this gift. One of the most simple is to recognize the meaning we have discovered for our own lives and help others discover meaning for theirs.

When my father-in-law, A. J. Metzler, was in his final year at a nursing center, he had a roommate who swore so badly we refrained from taking our grandchildren into the room. On one visit, I was surprised to discover A. J.'s roommate wasn't swearing but was instead visiting with his seventeen-year-old granddaughter. In one hand she had a newspaper clipping, in the other a cupcake with a bright pink candle.

"Grandpa," she said, showing him the clipping, "I brought a picture of your medal award ceremony from the Second World War."

The man sat up in bed and responded with only one swear word: "I was a pretty damned good soldier, wasn't I?"

"Yes," said the granddaughter, "and I've brought you a cake to celebrate how good you were—and that you are the world's best grandpa." A tear trickled down the old man's cheek as he reached out to embrace his grandchild. For several minutes he was focused, smiling, present, and, above all, in touch with one thing in his life that was worth celebrating.

Life is a gift. Life is to be celebrated now, not next week or next month or next year.

People of joy, celebrating life, are among the most grateful. They make phone calls, send cards or e-mails, and remember those aspects of their life worth celebrating. Certainly it is easier to be grateful and to celebrate when our needs are met, when health is good, and when we have what we need to carry on with the basic tasks of life. Yet people of joy are grateful even when circumstances are difficult.

Life is a gift!

— 2 —

Life Is Sacred

To the poet, to the philosopher, to the saint,

all things are friendly and sacred,

all events profitable, all days holy, all men divine.

—Ralph Waldo Emerson

Summer days had lots of possibilities for seven children on a farm. One day, two of my brothers joined me in the brooder house looking at the chicks that had hatched the day before. One brother —I'll not reveal who—suggested that, if we could hold a peep in one hand and bonk its head with a finger of the other hand, the dazed little chick should run around in circles. Neither of my brothers wanted to be the "bonker." So I was nominated to carry out the snap-the-peep-on-the-head experiment.

I grabbed the fluffy, yellow ball of fuzz and put him on my left palm. With my right middle finger aimed as if shooting a marble, I let it fly. But as I put the peep on the ground, I realized, to my horror, that it was dead. Apparently, I had broken its neck. I scooped the chick up as my brothers looked on in dismay. We were arguing about what to do next when Dad came around the corner of the chicken house.

"What happened to the peep?" he asked, looking at the pathetic little thing, its head drooping over my palm and its two little feet sticking straight up in the air.

"He fell over," I said, stalling to hold off what I was sure was to come.

"Why did he fall over?" Dad asked, looking me straight in the eye.

"I petted him too hard and he fell over," I said, easing away from my father.

"You killed him, didn't you?" Dad said.

"Uh huh," I replied, choking back tears of both sadness and fear.

Dad took my brothers and me over to a stump. I was sure I was about to get the pre-paddling lecture. I was shaking because I was familiar with the unpleasantness of Dad's hand-to-the-rump punishment. But this time it did not come.

Dad simply said, "Boys, you know we are nonviolent people. You know we do not hurt living creatures. We especially do not hurt each other. We see all of life as sacred and precious. So by hurting this little chick, you are violating everything we believe about nonviolence. Do you understand me?"

Again, a feeble "uh huh" from me. Dad's lecture ended with this conclusion: "Now, rats, cockroaches, and flies do not count."

Apparently we had not learned from previous experiences of harming living creatures—like my little brother. The event happened on our previous farm, the Hooley farm. The Hooley farm was particularly memorable because of all the wonderful buildings we could climb into or otherwise investigate. The ten-foot-by-ten-foot chicken house, with its nearly flat, tar-paper-covered roof, provided a unique challenge.

We three boys, Ronnie, Danny, and I, decided to scale the long barn pole that was leaning against the coop and protruding several feet above the roof. With considerable help from each other, we managed to find ourselves perched atop this wonderful lookout. We could see beyond the clover fields, over the barbed-wire fence, beyond the sled-riding hill, past the small bushes and pasture grass, all the way to the old swimming hole. It was glorious! Glorious, that is, until one day Ronnie and I got the bright idea that we could use the pole as a launch for Danny's arced trip to the ground.

As someone once said, "It seemed like a good idea at the time." We had convinced Danny that it would be safe for him to grab onto the pole, as it projected over the top of the roof, and we would simply give him and the pole a mighty push, and he could ride the arc of the pole to the ground. It still is not clear to me how we convinced him that this was a good idea, but we did.

He clung to the pole as we gave him the mighty shove we had promised. The scheme seemed to work, because he hung on for dear life as the pole made its projected trajectory to the ground. The problem was that Danny was on the side of this huge pole that first contacted the ground. Horrors!

He was motionless. No movement came from our little brother, nothing. We really did not mean to hurt him. To make matters worse, we had just jettisoned our only elevator to the ground. We were stranded, helpless, scared, and crying, as Danny began to stir. Apparently he'd had the wind knocked out of him, and it took a bit of coughing and sputtering to get his steady breath back again. And of course, he was way too small to erect the pole back to its ladder status. What to do, what to do?

The only option was to watch one little, battered boy cry his way to the house and retrieve our mother. After she had checked Danny for serious injuries and fortunately found little more than a knot on his head, she ran out of the house to see us sheepishly sitting on the chicken house roof. Needless to say, that evening was much longer than we had hoped for, in terms of lectures, scolding, and "come-upences" we so justly deserved.

After this chicken event and a scolding from Dad, I got the idea: life is sacred. (Killing chickens, Mom said later, was justified, when we used them to feed the family.) This sacredness of life we learned not only at home but also at church. Each person has a spark of life beyond the human body.

That spark is sacred. It can be found in every individual. No matter how vile or wicked or mean, each person has this sacred spark.

That's sometimes hard to believe. I remember the time when, working in the emergency room, I entered a room and saw something that took my breath away. A woman of about fifty was on the bed, her body's waste tangled in her mass of hair. As I turned her arm over to locate a vein for a blood sample, I saw black, gooey, tarry gunk, which actually moved—maggots, in her armpits and under her fingernails.

"Where is the sacred?" I asked myself. How could this woman, who had been sleeping in dumpsters, be called sacred? Yet as the physicians and aides worked over her to clean her up and make her more comfortable, I knew she was a human being like me. She had the sacred spark in her. No matter what choices she had made, no matter what her condition, she had that spark of sacredness. It is present in each of us.

People of joy consistently look for the sacred in others. Joy includes the ability to look past the circumstances, past the obnoxious or distasteful, to find the sacred spark. How we define *sacred* is not as important as is our ability to find the sacred in others. When this happens, we may find we are more tender, kind, and compassionate.

Life is sacred!

— 3 —

Life Is Difficult

Tough times do not last. Tough people do.

Difficult times are really quite relative. One of the farmhouses in which we lived had no central heating. Another house had no indoor plumbing other than a cast-iron hand pump with which to pump water. We kept warm by running up the stairs, jumping into bed with one or two brothers, piling on the blankets, and snapping the chin straps on our World War II leather helmets. Yes, we wore those soft, fur-lined, leather helmets to bed. It was a necessity, as the windows were not in any way sealed from the cold. It was not unusual to have small ridges of fresh snow on the inside of the window ledges when we woke in the morning. Often the first thing we'd hear was our father shaking the grate in the old Franklin stove that sat on the dining room floor, just beneath the grid-covered hole that served as our heat register. We would make a mad dash down the stairs, dragging our school clothes for the day, stand in front of the stove, and warm up enough to get ready.

Were these difficult times? Was it difficult to run to the out-house in the cold of winter? Was it difficult to shiver until one warmed up enough to go to sleep? Was it difficult to take baths in the old, round, metal bathtub that Mother would fill from the flattop, wood-burning stove in the kitchen? (Actually it was only tedious if you were the last one to use the tub, as Mother added a hot kettle of water after each bather). Was life tough in those days?

Memory has a way of dulling the difficult and elevating the grand. In a real sense, however, these were not tough times. Tough times are those times over which you have little or no control. Tough times are loss of life, chronic illness, abject poverty, war, violence, torture, and matters that are life threatening or life denying. We were inconvenienced, and at times quite uncomfortable, as we grew up in circumstances that were not exactly cushy. These were not, however, tough times. Tough times often involve real pain—emotional, physical, or both.

Pain is real. Times can be tough. People of joy understand this.

They do not tell others to cheer up, saying tomorrow may be better. People of joy realize that could be a lie. For many, tomorrow will not be better; poverty, chronic illness, pain, illiteracy, violence, and greed can affect lives in such a way that, no matter how positive people may approach life, tomorrow simply will not be better than today. For these people, joy may exist only in the deep, quiet self-understanding of what it means to be on earth and to live with integrity and courage.

Some suffering and pain we bring on ourselves. Lifestyle choices often contribute to lack of health and the resulting pain and suffering. Even then, to seek solely to find only good times in life is not the road to joy.

Joy comes when we help each other through the difficult times. It also comes when we have the courage to face what we sometimes think impossible. Come with me on two trips my wife, Joyce, and I took several years ago.

First we went to Nepal for a trekking adventure. The hiking was rigorous, even though the paths were clearly worn and deeply carved into the mountainside. We hiked nearly eight hours each day of the two-week climb.

My trouble began about six days into the trek. At about eight thousand feet, as we came around a bend in the path, there it was: a ledge approximately a hundred feet in length, about three feet wide, with a sheer drop of more than six hundred feet to the right. No guardrails, of course, and no trees to catch falling bodies.

I have acrophobia, a fear of heights. I froze. Sheer terror surged through my bones and settled into my stomach; sweat broke out on my palms and forehead. All I could think of doing was turning around and walking the four days back to where we had started.

Mon, our Sherpa, who was carrying my backpack, saw my frightful dilemma. He turned to me and said the four words that made all the difference: "We will help you."

Mon explained that I needed to face the mountain, to look to my right, along the ledge. "Do not look at your feet," he said. "They know where they are going. Instead look where your feet will be moving over the next few minutes. We will place our hands on your shoulders and guide you sideways along the ledge. Don't worry!"

"Don't worry," I said as I experienced a great urge to get down on my hands and knees and crawl. "Don't worry!" We slowly shuffled along the ledge, inch-by-inch, foot-by-foot, and finally made it around the corner of the mountain.

That's the first key to dealing with difficult times: accept help. I felt safe because someone had helped me. I had not really asked for that help, but Mon saw my need and responded.

But sometimes we do need to ask for help. Often that's difficult to do. We are so independent, so self-sufficient, and so eager to prove that we can do it ourselves that the last thing we consider is asking for help.

Other times, we may need to take action to avoid what makes life difficult.

Later that evening, as we sat around the dinner table, Mon said with a grin, "If you were frightened today, you should see what lies ahead for tomorrow."

"What? What's ahead?" I asked.

"Five more cliffs like today," Mon said. "Only they are worse!"

As I lay on my bamboo cot that night, I stared at the ceiling and wondered how I could possibly make it through ten more—five going, five returning.

"I am a grown man," I told myself. "I know my needs and fears. I can see the beautiful mountain peaks from here, and I do not need to make this trek through ten more cliffs." I finally dropped off to sleep at two a.m.

Next morning, when I told Joyce I had decided to stay in camp while the rest continued on for two more days, she surprised me by deciding to stay with me. We relaxed, played with the small band of local children at the camp, met fellow trekkers who were passing through, and generally had a safe and secure time.

When our party returned my brother-in-law said, "You made the right decision. There were some very scary places along the trail."

As people of joy, we do not always have to prove ourselves or do something we really do not want to do just to show how brave we are. Sometimes it is a good idea to say that we prefer not to put ourselves in harm's way.

At other times, courage comes because it is the only alternative.

In spite of my experience in Nepal, Joyce and I decided to celebrate our sixtieth birthdays by joining a group of college friends and hiking to the bottom of the Grand Canyon. The evening before, we went to an illustrated lecture about the hike. Halfway through the show, it became evident to me that there were, once again, ledges and cliffs.

I should have known that. But I had assumed that canyon paths simply go down along winding switchbacks, a rigorous but non-threatening hike to the bottom. So when we returned to our room, I suggested to Joyce that perhaps I should sit this one out.

She told me to sleep on it, and we would decide in the morning.

Morning arrived, and so did a card from Joyce. On the front was a boy, dressed in cowboy hat and boots, tears trickling down his cheeks. Above him, in large letters, were the words, "GET OVER IT." I opened the card and read, "It is just another birthday," but Joyce had crossed out "birthday" and substituted "hike." Joyce smiled as she squeezed my hand and gave me my water bottle.

She led the way, calling back every few minutes, "How's it going back there?" Step by step, we worked our way down the trail. I found it frightening on the one hand but awesome on the other. It certainly helped that someone thought I had enough courage to do it.

An hour after everyone else in our team had made it to the bottom and was feasting on steaks, Joyce and I walked into camp. We had made it! While this was, without a doubt, one of the most frightening days of my life, it also turned out to be one of the most exhilarating.

Sometimes courage is the only alternative to the difficulties of life. Think of those who live with HIV/AIDS or who inhabit drought-stricken lands in Africa. But even here we can say, "Can I walk with you down the canyon? Can I stand with you in your pain?"

People of joy know that life does have difficult times. They know that today may not be going very well. People of joy also know when to ask for help, to avoid doing what is unnecessarily dangerous, and to look for courage when they can't. It is about fellow travelers helping each other.

Life is difficult!

— 4 —

Life Is Short

I have learned that to be with those I like is enough.

—Walt Whitman

People of joy know that life is short. They know they do not have time to waste. For this reason, they continually update their opinion about what is meaningful. They ask, What is life about? What is fulfilling?

The answers do not lie in seeking pleasure, ease, comfort, or satisfaction. For me, they lie in investing time in building friendships. Friendships create a bank account that endures for a lifetime. Neither rust nor thieves can rob us of well-crafted, sincere, deep, life-long friendships. True friendships provide the savory sweetness of kinship and community. They give meaning to the short span of life.

How does one cultivate friendships? The stimuli for the following ideas are from the book *Caring Enough to Forgive* by David Augsburger.

1. Accept. People of joy understand that accepting others is essential to building friendships. And they know this acceptance must be genuine. If there is any sense of rich helping poor, smart helping dumb, or strong helping weak, that acceptance is seen for what it is: a fraud. True acceptance means being available to support, encourage, clarify, give feedback, learn from, and otherwise relate to another human being. Acceptance is about being fellow travelers, equals on a path toward friendship.

Sometimes that's difficult. It was for me with the purple-haired boyfriend.

When our daughter came down the stairs dressed for her first big dance, it was clear to me that she was beautiful, perfect, just right. Her boyfriend's arrival stole my breath for other reasons. He had on an orange tuxedo, accented with a green cummerbund. His black-and-white checkered tennis shoes seemed out of place. His hair had a streak of purple, his earring was a bit large, and his pigtail was slung forward over his shoulder.

"Accept, accept, accept," I said to myself. "Behave, father-of-the-young-and-beautiful-woman, behave; she could marry this fruitcake!"

It turns out that our daughter's date was one of most gentle, honest, caring, and clean-cut young men you would ever want to meet. Clearly, purple hair is not fatal! Acceptance goes well beyond physical appearance.

2. Be available. People of joy understand that friendship grows with availability. We can't be available to everybody all the time, but joyful friendship means we do have an in-depth commitment to a few. This means paying attention to friendship over a long period. It means that when we see imperfections in others we are still there for them. It means that they are still there for us when they see imperfections in us.

I grew up with four brothers, two sisters, and, oftentimes, one or two foster children. One of these foster children was Luci. She had a knack for getting into trouble. Whether it was swearing too much, running away from home, sneaking cigarettes, or going down to the basement to sneak my father's elderberry "medicine," she was good at it.

When Luci became an adult, she moved to the same city in which I lived. There she gave birth to three children fathered by three different men, none of whom lived with her. Luci supported herself with her welfare check and subsidized housing.

She also called me occasionally. One evening her request was, "Could you come and help me kill the rats?"

Rats! I hate rats. In fact, rats rank right up there with cliffs, in terms of my irrational fears.

Then Luci said, "My children sleep on mattresses on the floor, and during the night the rats come and bite them on the toes, and they bleed. It scares the children and me, and we have a terrible time sleeping. Please, can you come and help?"

What to do, what to do? "Of course I'll come," I mumbled, wondering if I shouldn't call the exterminator instead and just pay the bill. But I went, armed with four rat traps.

When I arrived, Luci gathered up her children and headed for the bedroom. I found a broom handle and began my fearful probing beneath the refrigerator and the stove. No rats. Then I headed to the bathroom, where I found a disposable diaper with a hole chewed in one side, obviously the work of a rodent.

In the basement, I located the source of the trouble. There was a hole at ground level in the window. It was a simple matter to plug the hole, cover it with duct tape, and set the rat traps for the intruders still inside.

The next morning Luci called to thank me. We had captured three rats.

Availability is a time to go, to be, and to do. Availability sometimes means going when we'd rather be doing other things. Availability is about loyalty and kindness.

People of joy understand the simple principle of being available.

3. Be authentic. People of joy understand that for friendships to grow, one needs to be authentic.

My mother was authentic. Her gentle, accepting, compassionate self was clear to all who met her. She had a welcoming, hospitable presence that brightened our home. (Dad made certain she was never short on guests to welcome!) In her gentleness, she had a disarming way of making visitors feel like she had been waiting, with glad anticipation, just for their arrival.

On the other hand, Mom's authenticity meant she wasn't afraid to say what she thought. She never liked my rebel-against-the-authorities, 1960s-style beard, which I have to this day. "When are you going to shave your beard?" she would inquire, a note of hope in her voice. But then she would add almost as an afterthought, "Oh well, it really doesn't matter, because I love you anyway."

And I knew she meant it.

On the other hand, her authenticity could be misguided. We were not permitted to go swimming on Sunday afternoons. Besides being the time when we would visit our grandparents in Orrville, it was supposed to be a day of noninvolvement in the work-a-day world. We refrained from buying gasoline and groceries on Sunday as well. But this thing about not swimming on Sunday, what possible reason could be given for such a dogma? Mom's answer was as curious then as it is in my memory: "What will people think if you drowned on a Sunday?"

People of joy know they need to be authentic in both family and community. If they have a passion for the poor, authenticity means doing something to help the poor. If they desire justice, authenticity means promoting those activities that bring forth justice.

4. Recognize. People of joy understand the importance of recognizing others' attempts at anything worth doing. Friendships grow as people feel affirmed and honored for what they are able to accomplish. Life is too short to let these opportunities pass us by.

We have a woman in our church for whom life has not been easy. Anita walks with a shuffle, which makes it difficult for her to walk quickly. Sometimes her speech is hard to understand. One Sunday morning during sharing time, Anita asked if she could read a poem. Slightly stooped, her hands fumbling with a piece of paper, she went to the microphone and read,

> Love is a beautiful thing.
> Let's spread it all over.
> Love is catching on.
> Let's pass it on, pass it on, pass it on!

For a moment the congregation sat silently as we recognized Anita's small steps into the world of poetry. It did not end there. Someone took the crumpled piece of paper and composed a song with those words. It is called "Anita's Song." Today, when Anita is a bit discouraged or when she just wants to celebrate, she stands up during sharing time and asks, "Will someone lead my song?" Then the congregation breaks into "Anita's Song" in four-part harmony, as we've been doing now for nearly thirty years.

5. Reinforce. Just as our church did with Anita, people of joy reinforce the potential they see in others. Small steps move bodies through space. Small steps, when recognized, encourage us to continue trying.

When I was in the third grade, there was an elderly woman who would greet me at church. She would actually get down on one knee and look me in the eye and say, "You're Jeppy aren't you?" This may not seem like much, but when a family has five boys, it becomes a task for acquaintances to tell the boys apart. The fact that this woman knew my name was positive recognition.

Further, she said, "I understand you can spell real well!"

To tell the truth, I did not know I was a good speller. It is not surprising that by the fifth grade I was up to competing in some serious spelling bees. I was never quite as good as she thought I was or even as good as I thought I was. But I did become a decent speller.

Although I think I look like a turtle inching along the pavement, I have run four marathons, the last of which was when I was sixty-five years old. Several days before my first one, I received this letter from Mom:

> Dear Jeppy,
> I understand that when you are training for the marathon, you like to memorize poetry. I remember when you were young you memorized over three hundred Bible verses so you could get a free trip to summer camp. I thought about that this morning and decided to send you the following Bible verses for you to consider memorizing. I'm praying for you as you run your marathon.
> Love, Mom.

Mom had handwritten a Bible verse for each letter of the alphabet. And she didn't even know a marathon is twenty-six miles long. With that reinforcement, I sat down and memorized a verse for each mile. What a distraction from the discomfort of running all twenty-six! (See appendix C for her list.)

6. Respect. People of joy respect others. They know that respect must be the basis for all friendship. They also know that respect brings dignity to all, no matter what their circumstances.

I walk the two miles to church as many Sundays as I can. Sometimes I leave early and stop by my granddaughters' house, picking up those of the three who want to walk with me. On the way, we often encounter a homeless person or two. Though I ordinarily don't contribute money to street beggars or homeless persons, on Sunday mornings I always put a dollar or two in my pocket, just in case.

In this way, we met Betty. One Sunday morning as we walked by the bagel shop, we looked in the window and saw an older woman eating breakfast by herself. One granddaughter asked, "Doesn't she have anyone to eat with?"

Another asked, "Do you think she is all alone in life?"

"Why don't we go in and meet her?" I asked. After a small bit of convincing, we walked in and introduced ourselves to Betty. We admitted we were complete strangers, but we thought she would be a fine woman to get to know. Now, every Sunday the girls wonder whether or not we will get to see Betty.

Perhaps it is no big deal. But my hope is that in this way, our granddaughters are learning respect for others. If they are to become people of joy, they must also be people who respect others, regardless of the person's station in life.

There's no time to do otherwise.

Life is short!

— 5 —

Life Is Funny

Look at the aardvark; that's all you need

to see the humor of life.

Life has its moments! Recently Joyce and I spent a week in the Pocono Mountains. One day, while she was out walking, I decided to go to the swim center to enjoy the Jacuzzi. When I arrived, I was pleased to see there were no other guests. I would have the hot tub to myself. I turned on the timer and lowered myself into the hot, three-foot-deep, clean, bubbly water. Aaaahhhhh!

"Ah, yes," I told myself, "this would be even better if I got rid of these shorts." After all, the attendant was way over there by the door, working on her books, and with the bubbles and all, neither she nor anyone else could see below the surface of the pool. So, dipping down to my neck, I slipped out of my red nylon running shorts that doubled for a swimsuit. How refreshing, sitting here in the Jacuzzi, enjoying the bubbles, not a care in the world. Nothing on, either.

But I was nervous. I thought perhaps I should practice returning my shorts to their designated place. To my chagrin, I realized that the bubbling action had twisted the inner lining into some kind of arrangement I could not get untangled. Even worse, the attendant started ambling in my direction. "No," I thought, "no, don't come over here." I knew she could not see below the surface of the water, but just the same, I quickly sat down and held the shorts over the area most vulnerable to exposure. How long did I set the timer for? What if it turned off and the water became still?

"Good morning," she said cheerfully, as she dipped little tubes into the pool to check the water.

"Good morning," I replied, trying to look nonchalant. She left. "Now," I said to myself, "I must get these shorts on." Too late! In came a woman, heading straight for my private Jacuzzi. I must get these shorts on now! Desperately I tried to untangle the mess. I had just completed the task and was ready to pull on the shorts when they slipped out of my grasp. I dove under the water, opened my eyes to a stinging chlorine bath, and managed to snag my shorts at the far side of the Jacuzzi. As fast as I could, I scampered back to a seat as far from the entrance steps as possible and struggled to slip on my shorts. Made it!

"Hi there," I said, "how are you today?"

I stood to leave the pool. That's when I discovered that, while I had somehow managed to get into my shorts, one of the legs was turned inside out, and the lining made a diagonal stripe down my leg. Quickly I sat down again. Working underwater, trying to look like nothing was happening, all the while smiling at my pool mate, I slid one leg out of my shorts, righted the problem, and put the offending side back on. Task completed, I slunk out of the pool and headed home.

It seemed like such a good idea at the time! People of joy use that phrase a lot. People of joy also know that the healthiest laughter comes from laughing at oneself.

There are many different kinds of laughter. Indeed laughter can be seen as a progression of spontaneous events.

Laughter starts with a *smile.* Hopefully, regardless of our circumstances, we all can smile now and then when a thing of beauty comes into our lives. The sound of music, whether produced by human or bird, can make us smile both inside and out. Cartoons, funny movies, jokes, and other word plays can do the same thing.

Smiling is one of the first forms of communication from a baby. Adults work hard to elicit a baby's first smile. In some traditions, the person who achieves this is responsible for throwing a big party for the baby and parents.

After the smile comes the twinkle. This involves more, including the corners of the eyes and the eyebrows. Sometimes even the forehead gets involved. A twinkle may be short-lived as we move into the next stage: the *giggle, titter,* or *chuckle,* depending on personality type. Some folks will never titter, but they will gladly giggle or chuckle.

Giggling can lead to increasingly infectious laughter. This laughter has many forms, sounds, and expressions. The diaphragm and larynx contribute to a complex exhalation or spontaneous explosion of what can often be really weird sounds. Some folks even snort, as laughter takes over the entire breathing system. Laughter can be as loud or as quiet as the person to which it belongs.

And then, depending on a person's willingness to "let go," there's the *belly laugh*. A person in this state is often out of control, with eyes shut, head tipped back, and belly jiggling with riotous laughter. Belly laughs are invariably shared; a solo belly laugh is rare. When a belly laugh takes over, little can stop the eight to ten seconds it takes to "let off steam."

A belly laugh often leads to *crying*. The tears flow from the wonderful release of "letting go." One literally laughs until crying. At this stage, some slap others on the back, make kicking motions, swagger around the room, maybe nearly fall down.

That's the adult version. Children, on the other hand, can move right into a form of laughter I call ROFL (Rolling On the Floor Laughing). Adults rarely succumb to this kind of expression of laughter, but some have been known to do so, including the monk and author Thomas Merton. This is the ultimate in out-of-control laughter. It's a cathartic release from the tensions and stress that can accompany the heaviness of life.

Yet laughter is not for everyone. We have two main influences on our ability to laugh: upbringing and genetics. As a result, most of us find ourselves on a laughter continuum ranging from rarely

allowing ourselves to laugh (1) to permitting ourselves to laugh
with reckless abandon (10).

Dour, cautious, pessimistic					*Lighthearted, spontaneous, upbeat*				
1	2	3	4	5	6	7	8	9	10
Little permission to laugh						*Great permission to laugh*			

*Locate your position on this continuum. Are you more serious,
cautious, or even pessimistic, or are you more lighthearted, spontaneous, and upbeat? Are other members of your immediate family
at the same place?*

Each of us comes with a unique background that affects how
much permission we give ourselves to participate in humor. For
example, a child raised in an atmosphere of devastation, with mental,
physical, or sexual abuse, is likely to have a hard time appreciating
that healthy humor or lighthearted living. Humor is foreign to that
child's experience. An unhappy childhood makes it difficult to
appreciate the various modalities of laughter when one reaches
adulthood.

On the other hand, a happy, well-adjusted home, where humor
and laughter are abundant, gives children permission to participate
in humor events. A child from such a home will be familiar with
harmless practical jokes, laughter, joke telling, and mirth. Such a
child is likely to take himself or herself less seriously. This child is

more likely to have a good sense of humor, to participate readily in laughter, and to understand humor.

Sense of Humor

What does it mean when we say someone has a "good sense of humor"? This is an interesting question when one realizes that a sense of humor is one of the most desired character attributes when seeking a prospective mate. The term "sense of humor" is most likely highly specific to the person making the statement. For example, if one was raised in a family where sarcasm was seen as humor, then sarcastic humor is seen as the norm. On the other hand, if practical jokes were a part of one's experience, then a person who enjoys, participates in, or is the brunt of harmless practical jokes—and is a good sport about it—can be seen as a person with a good sense of humor.

Still others see a sense of humor as an attribute of those who laugh well, who have an easy smile, and who are not afraid to participate in all-out belly laughing. Then there are those who are actually skilled at telling a joke. With excellent timing, they remember the punch line, and they can deliver it with the surprise ending that is needed.

Puns, oxymorons, and riddles are also a part of the picture. They are often called "groaners," and they are cherished in some families much more than others. A person of wit can also be seen as a person with a sense of humor. Even a person who enjoys "clowning" is seen as a person with a sense of humor.

The list of sense-of-humor styles can be quite extensive, but it would not be complete without the ubiquitous "dry" sense of humor. This dryness is family-defined, culturally bound, and definitely in the eye of the beholder.

When I ask people if they have a sense of humor, the answer is tied to what they perceive this to mean. In other words, they relate to a *specific type* of sense of humor. They see themselves as having attributes that relate to one or more of the following:

1. Enjoying sarcastic humor
2. Participating in harmless practical jokes
3. Laughing easily
4. Being able to tell a joke
5. Welcoming puns, oxymorons, riddles
6. Having wit
7. Clowning
8. Having a dry sense of humor

Look at the list above and ask the question, "Do I have a sense of humor?" How would you describe your own understanding of this characteristic? What was your family like? Where did you learn about humor? What shape has your sense of humor taken?

A good sense of humor can include enjoying harmless, practical jokes, with the emphasis on *harmless*. To understand the story of the following practical joke, one needs to understand the construction of the stairs at one of my childhood homes. The same farmhouse that had the Franklin stove had a wooden staircase with a door at its entrance. This door served to keep the heat from going upstairs needlessly and helped contain it in the dining room.

One of my older brothers, John, was about eight years my senior, so when I was ten he was around eighteen, just right for dating. Like most young men, he enjoyed driving the car and taking prospective suitors home from hymn sings or socials or whatever happened to be going on that particular evening. He had a curfew of eleven p.m., at which time he was supposed to be home. Often Mother and Dad would lie awake (their bedroom was on the first floor, just feet away from the Franklin stove) until our dating brothers (and later us) would come home. They would quiz us about how things went, where we went, and whether we had a good time. On other occasions, they would fall asleep, and curfews could be circumvented.

On this particular night, John was apparently going to be late, and he was going to try to sneak in quietly past the bedroom door, tiptoe up the wooden stairs, and slither into bed. Several of us brothers and a tag-along little sister decided to set a trap. It was a simple operation to fill a metal coal bucket with husked, dried, black walnuts, and place it at the top of the wooden steps. The trigger device was an appropriate length of binder twine (used in the baler to bind hay bails) with one end tied to the bucket handle and the other tied to the doorknob at the bottom of the steps. With the trap set, we could all go to bed, knowing we would certainly know when John arrived home.

A bucket of walnuts being emptied down the wooden staircase served as a wonderful alarm clock for the entire household.

We still have a good laugh today when we remember this practical joke.

We must also realize that not all of life is funny. There are times when we can legitimately carry the weight of the world on our shoulders. Laughter can also be used as avoidance. Families may use humor to get around having to deal with serious matters, confrontation, or pain.

Yet most of us can learn to laugh. "Someday I'll laugh about this," we sometimes say. Why not start now? For the person of joy, there is no shortage of times for laughter and humor.

Life is funny!

— 6 —

Life Is a Spiritual Journey

Every moment and every event of every man's

life on earth plants something in his soul.

—Thomas Merton

In 1997, I traveled to Calcutta for the Mennonite World Conference. Sitting, singing, and praying with several thousand brothers and sisters, celebrating our common faith, was quite significant to me. That trip took on even deeper meaning when I was able to have an extended conversation with a man I consider to be a person of great spiritual wisdom and depth. His words encouraged me to nurture my soul, follow my inner voice, and celebrate the journey. The conversation was a moment of spiritual renewal.

Later that same afternoon, I met a local artist, Leela Lall. While displaying her artwork and talking about her life, she held up a beautiful wooden plate that had a fish in the center made out of broken pieces of tile and glass. I was drawn to that plate. Not only is the fish a symbol of Christianity, for me it was also a sign of the spiritual encouragement I had just received.

I had to have that plate. It spoke to me; it was an emblem of the day's journey. So, following Leela's presentation, I asked, "Would there be any chance you would be willing to sell that plate?"

She smiled, seemingly pleased that I liked her work. Much to my shock, she said she was asking 1,200 dollars. My heart sank. That was way beyond my limited budget. Then Leela corrected herself; she was talking about rupees, not dollars. The price in U.S. dollars was less than thirty.

I bought the plate, took it over to the shade of a nearby tree, sat down, and pulled it out of the bag. I wept. Somehow, in some mysterious way, the day had brought together the wisdom of a spiritual mentor and the beauty and meaning of an artisan's plate.

I wept because I came in touch with the fact that life is a spiritual journey. Sometimes we simply do not understand the beauty and encouragement present in special moments. There is a mystery to this journey. Even today this plate continues to remind me how great a desire I have to nurture my innermost being.

People of joy take time to nurture themselves. They take time to enrich their souls, spirits, and minds. Life is a journey, a journey that requires the nurturing of one's inner being.

Don't Just Do Something, Sit There

One could say that spirituality is as simple, yet as complex, as the active pursuit of meaning in one's life. For some, spirituality involves a higher power, whether within or without an organized religion. For others, who might not include a higher being in the equation, spirituality can be enhanced through music, meditation, art, an awareness of nature, or other ways of nurturing the being. At the very least, spirituality involves principles, values, and circumspection regarding how one "is" in this world.

This pursuit of spirituality can include humor, which seems to be beneficial to us humans. We are not certain how it all works together, but it seems reasonable to assume that to be at one's healthiest best, one must at the very least nurture the mind, the soul, and the heart.

A key to spiritual health is finding the avenue of nurturing that best fits your own style and that works best for you. In general, one person's path may not fit everyone else. At the same time, there are some common threads that involve those things in life that give you a sense of well-being, strength, inner peace, celebration, love, and nurturing relationships with others.

The Difference Between Feeling Good and Doing Good

The search for possibilities beyond ourselves begins simply. I call it SDSU: Sit Down and Shut Up. For many of us, the fast orbits of our lives makes it difficult to stop—turn off the answering machine, the television, the computer, the e-mail—and simply be still, and listen.

This somewhat tongue-in-cheek admonition to sit down and

shut up is a way of saying that we should take time each day to do at least one thing that moves us toward spiritual growth. Some use meditation, others prayer, some sing songs or listen to their favorite music or go for long walks in nature. Still others find solace in reading, participating in sports, or attending religious services.

Obviously Eastern religions have a long tradition of meditation, which can certainly be a way to approach spirituality. Centering, freeing, relaxing, timeless meditation can give us the deep quiet that rests the inner mind and spirit.

For some, music provides nourishment for the soul, and listening to music that especially speaks to them can be a way to nourish the inner being. The same can be said for quiet recreation, such as fishing, walking, birding, and other activities in nature.

When I think of people who have their lives "together," who exhibit the qualities of the deep joy to which we all aspire, I find they are people who take time to nurture themselves. They may do it through books, by sharing their spiritual journey with others, or by participating in worship, prayer, or meditation. They may even nurture themselves through service to others. The inward journey can be approached by a myriad of routes. No matter. What's important is that we still find time to nurture ourselves.

People of joy do not just skate through life with a six-pack and a remote control. They pay attention to their brains, their spirits, and their souls. Without this drive to expand horizons, to widen views, to encounter new wonders, and to truly be alive, the person of joy is incomplete.

Life is a spiritual journey!

Part II

Becoming People of Joy

— 7 —

Cultivating Humor

"How do we become people of joy?" I am often asked. That is both an easy and a difficult question to answer. There are so many different ways to joy, probably as many ways as there are people.

One thing I have found helpful, however, is to cultivate humor. To help people do just that, I've created what I call the Hostetler Humor Index and the Hostetler Humor Umbrella. We'll consider each in this and the next chapter.

I encourage you to complete both the adolescence and current indexes in this chapter. Score them and discuss the surprises or reinforcement of remembrances you already have about your early and later humor permission. Use the questions at the end to compare the results from different stages of your life: adolescent then adult.

Do not take yourself too seriously as you fill out the forms. Respond with the first impression that comes to your mind.

The Hostetler Humor Index

Adolescence

I developed this index to help you assess your background, upbringing, permission to laugh, and your tendency to be lighthearted. In the blanks below, rate yourself on a scale of 1 to 5 according to the following:

1—never or rarely; 2—occasionally; 3—sometimes; 4—quite often; 5—almost always

During my childhood and adolescence:

1. ____ I had permission to laugh out loud.
2. ____ I can remember specific incidences when I laughed out loud.
3. ____ My mother or adult female caretaker laughed out loud.
4. ____ My father or adult male caretaker laughed out loud.
5. ____ Our family had a sense of humor, either noisy or quiet.
6. ____ There was a sense of optimism in our family.
7. ____ We celebrated birthdays, anniversaries, and other significant milestones.
8. ____ We had a pet in our home.
9. ____ I enjoyed harmless, practical jokes.
10. ____ We sang, danced, or played together, partially or as a family.

11. ____ Mealtime was a fun time at our house.
12. ____ We ate ice cream or other comfort foods.

Total this section (items 1-12): _____ (scores will range from 12 to 60)

Results, according to your total:

12-24 You had little permission to participate in humor events.
25-36 You had a fair amount of permission to participate in humor events.
37-48 You had a moderate amount of permission to participate in humor events.
49-60 You had a great deal of permission to participate in humor events.

Current

This index was created to assess your current permission and tendency to participate in events that produce humor. In the blanks below, rate yourself on a scale of 1 to 5 according to the following:

1—never or rarely; 2—occasionally; 3—sometimes; 4—quite often; 5—almost always

As an adult today:

13. ____ I enter into "play" with children or adults.
14. ____ I join in the celebration of significant events.
15. ____ My movie diet includes funny movies.
16. ____ In the theater, I laugh out loud at funny scenes.
17. ____ I read cartoons, comic books, or "funny papers" whenever I find them.
18. ____ I laugh out loud at newspaper or other printed cartoons or funny stories.
19. ____ I tend to tell jokes when I can remember the punch line.
20. ____ I enjoy hearing a good joke, one-liner, or pun.
21. ____ I believe I have a sense of humor.
22. ____ I enjoy a good belly laugh.
23. ____ I am basically an optimistic person.
24. ____ I like to sing, dance, yodel, whistle, or hum.

Total this section (items 13-24): _____ (scores will range from 12 to 60)

Results, according to your total:

12-24 You do not give yourself much permission to participate in humor events.

25-36 You give yourself a fair amount of permission to participate in humor events.

37-48 You give yourself a moderate amount of permission to participate in humor events.

49-60 You give yourself a great deal of permission to participate in humor events.

Now that you've completed both humor indexes, take a moment to reflect on what you have learned about yourself. Ask yourself these questions:

As an adolescent:

1. Does your score match what you thought your childhood memories were like with regard to humor, laughter, jesting, and celebration?
2. Do you think the adolescent index has any accuracy as you compare it to your own opinions?

3. Does your score on the adolescent index reflect an open system in your early childhood, that is, one in which you had permission to celebrate and laugh, or does it reflect a more closed way of approaching humor and humor events?

As an adult:

1. Do you think you have changed from those adolescent years?
2. How have you changed?
3. Is your appreciation and understanding of humor events at a different level than when you were an adolescent?
4. What is your appreciation of humor and mirth in your current situation?

Indexes like these are only one measure of how a person approaches joy and humor. It is important to remember that genetics also may play a role in your humor make-up. Some researchers suggest that genes may predispose a person to being lighthearted or to being dour. In other words, some folks have an inborn tendency to be more resilient, lighthearted, optimistic, buoyant, effervescent, and spontaneous. Others tend to be less resilient, lighthearted, buoyant, and optimistic.

The combination of one's upbringing and humor experiences in his or her background coupled with one's genetic predisposition toward light-heartedness or dourness contributes to the kind of humor work one is capable of doing.

— 8 —

Humor Work

When I began looking at humor as a positive force that augments healing, I was influenced by the anecdotal writings of Norman Cousins, who asked probing questions regarding the efficacy of laughter in the healing process. *Anatomy of an Illness as Perceived by the Patient* trumpeted his personal success in using laughter to overcome illness. This early book challenged many of us who were looking for the positive aspects of humor on healing.

Although the book gave no scientific proof for the power of laughter, it stirred the imagination and promoted research in an evolving field, psychoneuroimmunology (PNI). Cousin's follow-up book, *Head First: The Biology of Hope and the Healing Power of the Human Spirit* began to suggest possible scientific bases for the positive contributions hope, humor, and laughter have on the immune system and consequently on overall health.

Since the early 1990s, the National Institutes of Health and numerous psychology researchers have put together preliminary evidence for the positive nature of humor and hope. But this early work relating humor to positive influence on the immune system has not been replicated in large-scale studies. Books abound, many of which were pivotal in spurring my interest in the PNI field. Christian Hageseth's *A Laughing Place* was ahead of the pack. Paul Pearsall's *Super Joy* was also a part of the collective push to take seriously the matters of joy, hope, and humor. (See appendix A for a selective reading list.)

Of particular note is a series of books by a child-becoming-youth writer who died at the early age of fourteen. Mattie Stepanek, best known for the wisdom of his "Heartsongs" writings, appeared on *Oprah Winfrey Show*, *Larry King Live*, and numerous other national television programs. His early poetry (written as early as three years old) was dictated to his mother. The wisdom and exuberance of his writing came at a time when the "positive psychology" research was starting to blossom. Mattie's writings have uncanny insights into the joy of living, the celebration of life, and the promotion of peace and hope. I recommend them highly to anyone interested in finding ways to become more exuberant about life.

Now that you've taken the humor index assessments, you are ready to consider what it means to do humor work. How can you move from the more dour side of life to one of spontaneous, joyful exuberance that includes mirthful play, joke telling, celebrating, even clowning?

The Hostetler Humor Umbrella

There are so many ways to instigate healthy humor events. And because there are so many, one or two are bound to fit each person's history or genetic predisposition, no matter where he or she starts. I have gathered these in what I call the Hostetler Humor Umbrella. Under this umbrella is a collection of things you can do to cultivate humor and bring joy. It is not exhaustive, and I encourage you to consider some additional possibilities, like dance, music, and art.

1. Laugh. One kind of humor work is inviting others to laugh. Everyone can cultivate this ability. Reflect on your childhood or on a more recent life experience. Enjoy those silly knock-knock jokes. Share funny cartoons or send funny cards. In these ways, we can not only enjoy laughter ourselves but also bring it to others.

The truth is, however, that some people are simply not funny. They cannot remember punch lines. Or they laugh too hard before they get there. They may ruin or diminish the timing. I call them "joke-telling challenged." This is not good or bad; it just is. These people would be better served choosing other options for doing humor work.

Of course, if you are one of these joke-telling-challenged folks, you could use it to your advantage. If you're willing, others can get a kick out of hearing you tell jokes because you do it so badly. "Here comes Uncle Charlie," they say. "Get him to tell you the joke about the man who goes into the bar, sits down, and sees another man with a duck under his arm." Everyone knows the punch line, and everyone knows how badly you are going to mess it up. That's what makes it such fun, if you can take it.

There are many forms of creating laughter beyond joke telling. Comedians use one-liners, word pictures, contrasts, surprises, sight gags, puns, and all sorts of word play to invite laughter. Bill Cosby simply sits on a stool and tells stories that invite us into common experiences, sometimes leaving us laughing uncontrollably.

Some people get a kick out of seeing high-quality clowns. They are led to laugh when someone puts on a rubber nose or does a sight gag. Then there are the funny tricks we learned as children, the ones that make us known as the person who does the take-off-your-thumb trick.

Others have a quick wit and can insert surprise witticisms into a conversation or may have a humorous way of turning a phrase. Still others are good punsters, even though punning often brings more groans than laughter.

I take great delight in the humor of magic. I find it fun to put together story lines that involve touches of magic, often with funny endings. One of my trademarks, the cow-to-chicken trick, involves rolling a hand towel in a special way. (You'll find this trick in the appendix D for your use and enjoyment.)

Laughter clubs are being established all over the world today. People get together and—without such things as jokes, cartoons, or other funny starters—simply laugh together for thirty to forty-five minutes. It is catching. Participants say it is not only therapeutic but also a great deal of fun. It is certainly not for everyone, but some of us may be good candidates for laughter clubs.

The ultimate form of laughter is when we laugh at ourselves. We often hear the phrase, "Someday we are all going to laugh about this." My question is, why wait until someday? Why not begin laughing right now and get more mileage out of the situation? Okay, so it is difficult to laugh when you are right in the middle of a trying experience, but it is a good idea to think about ways to lighten up when it comes to taking ourselves too seriously.

Recently friends of mine related a story about how their son had just learned to drive. He was given permission to use the car to go to the church softball game that evening with the explicit instructions that he was not to take any passengers with him. As the evening progressed, our friends found themselves at a local ice-cream shop that had windows all around the building and wide, cement cruising lanes. As they were enjoying their hot-fudge goodies, they glanced up to see their son touring the parking lot with a young woman by his side. He seemed to be proud as a peacock to be able to sport this young woman around with his newly earned skills as a driver.

The son was unfortunate enough to meet the eyes of his parents. Oooops!

"Quick," he said to his female passenger, "duck down so my parents can't see you." It was too late. What to do, what to do? Clearly the day of reckoning was at hand. (Don't you just hate it when something like this happens to you?)

When the parents arrived home, young driver son was waiting in the living room. He faced the music, took his disciplinary stripes, and decided against future indiscretions in this particular venue. It was indeed a bad day. Ugh!

Years later, the son recounts this story with a great deal of fanfare, embellishment, and humor. The extended family gets a genuine hoot out of the story as they laugh until tears come to their eyes. "Someday we will laugh about this" has become "today" and the family enjoys hearing the episode being retold.

Stories of embarrassing situations, when told on one's self and understood by the gathered audience, are solid fodder for the laughter mill. We often discover that others have had similar situations happen to them, and the strength of humor lies in the shared experience or identification with the contents of the story. This is one reason comedian Bill Cosby is funny to so many people. He tells his stories with a great deal of embellishment and exaggeration, and even adds sounds and descriptions that capture the imagination. In them we find much in common with our own experiences.

Embarrassing situations can be turned into funny stories. All it takes is time, a sense of humor, and an imagination. Why not resurrect some of your past embarrassments and share them with your small group, your children, or your grandchildren? Couched with a tongue-in-cheek approach and announced with a cover of uncertainty as to the exact details, I can assure you that especially the grandchildren will enjoy hearing about your past foibles.

A word of caution is in order. There is healthy humor, and there is harmful humor. Healthy humor is inviting and forgiving, never hurtful. Healthy humor events will never hurt any segment of the population, any ethnic or religious group, or any profession. Not that you can't have great humor at the expense of a particular closed group. For example, a group of nurses can tell nurse jokes, a group of attorneys can tell jokes about lawyers, and, in my case, a group of Mennonites can tell jokes about Mennonites. The key is permission of the group.

2. Celebrate. Humor work can involve the simple act of helping another person celebrate a meaningful or exciting moment in life. Knowing a person well enough to discover the passions important to his or her life, we can create a card, obtain a gift, plan a surprise, or otherwise join in celebrating that person's particular joy. Doing so may even resurrect a memory or a way of being that may have seemed lost.

When Joyce and I were preparing for a two-month trip to India and Nepal, we had some doubts about leaving her aging father, A. J. Metzler, who had had a stroke some months earlier and was confined to a wheelchair. The right side of his body no longer responded to commands from his brain, his speech was nearly indecipherable, and his recognition of family members was limited, at best.

With this in mind, we made one of our frequent visits to see A. J., thinking this might be the last time Joyce saw her beloved father alive. She carefully cradled his left hand between her two hands and said, "Dad, Jep and I are going to go on a long trip very soon. We will be gone for about two months. We will be visiting Ed and Ethel in Nepal and the Millers in India."

No response. She continued, "Dad, do you mind if we go for that length of time?"

There was still no response. And then she asked, "May we have a prayer for you, and for us, before we go?"

With that, A. J. slowly lifted his head, and in words that were quite recognizable, he said, "I'll pray." He launched into a prayer for our safety, for Joyce's brother Ed and his wife Ethel, and for our safe return. He also prayed for people and churches that he had visited in India decades ago. Then he drifted off into a prayer about revival meetings and other things we could not understand.

We had tapped into the center of what A. J. Metzler was all about—his intense spirituality. His Christian faith was clear, steady, and, above all, recognizable as the way he actually lived. Somehow our asking about prayer caused him to tap into the roots that went way back to his younger days, underpinnings that were reinforced over an entire lifetime. He was at home with prayer. He could celebrate, even in his fog, the very essence of who he was.

I have a good friend who has a celebration calendar in her kitchen. On it are all the birthdays, anniversaries, and other significant events in her friends' and relatives' lives. Her greeting card budget is larger than most people's charitable giving for an entire year. Like clockwork, she carefully selects just the right card and writes a word of congratulations or encouragement on each card. She knows how to help people celebrate significant events in their lives. This is her gift to untold people, her way of cultivating joy. This is her humor work.

Regardless of age or abilities, all of us can find celebration moments for other people. It is a matter of choosing to get to know people and finding out what is meaningful to them. Celebration is, in the best sense, humor work. It tends to cheer people up. It brings back fond memories. One doesn't have to have a sense of humor or tell a joke in a funny way in order to celebrate.

3. Play. Play is often seen as the domain of children. But play is also possible for adults, when we suspend our notions of control of everything from how we look and behave to how we are perceived by others. Playfulness is humor work that invites people into the arena of "letting go" or the zone of suspended taboos. Playfulness is the ability to participate in childlike events without apology and without embarrassment.

Part of the reticence to play comes from a loss of spontaneity. My father said to me on at least one occasion: "Jeppy, you are like a frog. You jump up in the air, and while you are up there you look around to see if there is anyplace to land." I called that spontaneity; he called it impulsiveness.

I believe spontaneous people tend to have a lot more fun than nonspontaneous ones. We spontaneous ones use the phrase, "It seemed like a good idea at the time," a lot more than those less bombastic types.

As a faculty member, I once attended a university-sponsored workshop on being playful. The instructor had placed several large beanbag-type seats around the room. Our first assignment was to remove our shoes, neckties, and jackets and follow her instructions in a touching game. The idea was very simple: get down on the floor and touch one body part to that of another person, for example, your elbow to another person's knee. As the instructor called out the simple instructions, it soon became clear that several other male faculty members were having a very difficult time getting into the game. I was having a blast! The difference was one of upbringing and, I would guess, genetics.

Some folks simply do not have the ability to participate in childlike events. Playfulness is not the kind of humor work that appeals to all adults. But for those of us to whom it does appeal, it becomes a great way to cultivate joy.

3. Build hope. For a time, I was a career teacher in substance abuse. At my very first training session, I learned that you can't make anyone quit drinking or using drugs. You can only offer the hope of "one day at a time."

The same thing is true about humor. You cannot make people laugh. You can, however, offer a bit of hope. This is not some kind of wishful thinking, pie-in-the-sky inspirational fluff; it is standing with a person on the journey. It means encouragement in guarded measures, one day at a time. This is one of the keys to the success of twelve-step programs.

Hope building is truly humor work. It is giving people the affirmation and encouragement that gladdens the heart.

4. Be kind. Kindness is humor work that momentarily recognizes the other as a person of worth. Being kind includes recognizing that another person deserves consideration. It means taking the time to make things a bit better for another person.

To me it's not surprising that when we see kindness offered in difficult situations, we are somewhat incredulous. When there are long lines of cars trying to get out of a parking garage and the man in the blue car waves you into line, that kindness simply feels good.

With seven grandchildren coming and going in our house, we attempt to point them in the direction of kindness, reinforcing the same encouragement they receive from their parents. Joyce will often say to the grandchildren, "Don't forget to do one random act of kindness today." I also hear her admonishing them to play with that new student who is all alone or to sit with the child that others ignore. Be kind!

Being kind is one type of humor work we can practice wherever we go, wherever we are, in any country in the world. Kindness has no language barriers. It shows up when waiting in line to board a plane, when someone drops packages, and when seats are limited and an elderly person gets on the bus.

Practicing kindness will make kindness a habit. While putting others first is not exactly the norm in western civilization, attempting to do at least one act of kindness per day will go a long way toward cultivating joy.

5. Love. What's love got to do with humor? Everything! Nothing can cheer a person's soul more than knowing that he or she is truly loved.

Joyce is a registered nurse and a psychiatric nurse specialist. She has an uncanny ability to extend unconditional love to persons in trouble. She was in charge of an adolescent alcohol and other drug treatment center for a number of years. Early on, one of the rules stated that the professional team "is not permitted to touch the client." Being a mother and a compassionate nurse, she felt obligated to lobby the powers that be to get the rule changed. It seemed reasonable to her that, with permission and at the right time and place, a client should get a good, needed hug.

Since she worked with teenage girls, it became evident that genuine expressions of love would be therapeutic. It should be understood that when she would invite one of the girls to come to her, she would open her arms wide, and simply say, "Come here." She would enfold her in her arms and rock her gently back and forth, saying something like, "You know your behavior really stinks." Then she'd add, "But guess what, I think we can find a way out of this mess."

For some of Joyce's clients, it was the first time they had ever been hugged by an adult female. This is love in action, compassion at its best. This is, in the broad sense, humor work.

Perhaps this kind of humor work is most visible among family members and in some types of communities. But wouldn't our world be a far better place if love and compassion were the norm for all—from the people in the towns and cities where we live to the leaders in governments in countries around the world?

To love is also cultivating joy.

6. Practice hospitality. Practicing hospitality isn't always easy. But the beauty of being present with others over a cup of coffee or a meal can be most rewarding, both for hosts and for guests. Practicing hospitality is cultivating joy.

Dad and Mom thought a farm would give their seven children, several foster children, and a recovering alcoholic or two the space they needed to learn, grow, and understand how to be in this world. I do not imagine we had more than a hundred acres on any of the farms where we lived. The idea behind the "farm life" was to give us five boys and two girls something constructive to do. So we spent our growing-up years on rented farms: the Miller farm, the Hooley farm, and the Yoder farm. We did the best we could to try to farm, milk ten or twelve cows every morning and evening, sow and harvest crops, and maintain a large garden, which meant we'd be busy during the summer, canning vegetables and fruits.

The fruits of our labor were to be shared, particularly with folks who came to dinner. The meal was usually a Sunday noon meal, right after church. We invited a variety of folks to join us for stew, fresh sweet corn, tomatoes, squash, and a few vegetables that I still have a hard time identifying.

The tradition has been carried into my own adult life. We believe that hospitality is one of the best gifts one can give to strangers and friends alike.

Our interaction with prisoners, especially incarcerated men, grew out of our interest in those for whom life was not so fortunate. One such person was Henry. Henry was a tall, slender man, who had been in jail for eight years by the time we met him. He was the first African-American man our daughters had ever met. Often Henry's mother, Annie, would come to our house for the evening meal, now appropriately called "dinner." We enjoyed her company, and we enjoyed her sweet-potato pie.

Over dinner one evening, Annie asked if she could say the blessing. Of course, we assured her, we would welcome it. Annie began, "Dear Lord, when we all get to heaven it will be all howdy howdies and no goodbyes. Thank you, Jesus!" Her prayer went on, as she gently rocked forward and backward, blessing the food, the relatives, the president, world leaders, the local churches and their pastors, and especially her sick friends, for whom she requested, "And dear Lord, be with all my sick friends, just prop 'em up on the leanin' side." I smiled inside, delighting in the beauty of this prayer.

These words will forever be in my memory bank. "Just prop 'em up on the leanin' side." Sometimes we tend to want the world at our disposal and our pleas and supplications to God are grand and complete. We want everything fixed, cured, better, and just plain well. Annie's humble request says it best. I'm not asking a whole lot here, Lord, and I don't really want to be presumptuous, so a 'prop up' would do just fine right now, thank you.

Ervin Smith was a frequent visitor at my parents' home. After we children had moved out, Mom and Dad had an empty nest, which they gladly shared with visitors like Ervin.

Ervin was a miner. His skin was etched with coal dust, and his hands and fingernails were permanently black. He would come into the kitchen, light a cigarette, and enjoy cup after cup of coffee Mom would serve him. He did not have much to say, other than to tell a few stories everyone had already heard a dozen times or more. Sometimes he would make excuses for his drinking or he would ask for money.

Mom and Dad welcomed Ervin with unconditional love. Certainly they would have preferred him to arrive sober, and they hoped they could find him help. When he was sitting at their kitchen table, however, he was treated as a special guest. This is hospitality I understand.

This same hospitality was present in the Metzler home. Alta Metzler was frequently called upon by her well-known husband to prepare meals on short notice, get beds ready for international visitors, and to welcome all to her home. She did this with style and grace.

Hospitality is no doubt, one of the best ways to do humor work.

— 9 —

Things You Can Do
to Cultivate Joy

In this book, we've touched on what it means to be persons of joy. I trust that what I've included here has helped to increase your sense of joy. But what are some practical things you can do to make humor, spontaneity, lightheartedness, and laughter a part of your life?

Here are a few suggestions that might help move you in those directions:

1. Take time to stop and reflect on the events of your life that contributed to your own understanding and expression of joy.
2. Share your memories and stories with others. Do it with integrity, juiciness, and tenderness. Share them with grandchildren, children at church, civic gatherings, neighbors, and (sparingly, of course) at reunions, wedding receptions, and memorial celebrations.

3. Find treasured moments in your life to celebrate. Get out the photo albums you have not opened for years. Dig out the writings and art of your children, grandchildren, or special friends. Review the small trips you have made. Celebrate.
4. Gather some friends or family and take the two Hostetler Humor Indexes together. Then talk about what you have learned about yourself and about each other.
5. Select one or two options from the Hostetler Humor Umbrella and try to use what you've selected to bring joy to others.
6. Practice one act of kindness per day for a week. If you like what happens to you and to others, consider doing so on a more regular basis, until it becomes a great habit.

Become a person of joy!

Appendix A

Additional Resources and Bibliography

Further study

Positive psychology, as a field of serious scientific study, is relatively new and includes research into subjects such as hope, spirituality, mindfulness, gratitude, and optimism. The field brings attention to the major positive emotions. Courses can include gratitude and forgiveness, feeling good versus doing good, and why some people have hope and others have very little hope.

One of the leading departments where positive psychology is scientifically pursued is the Positive Psychology Center at the University of Pennsylvania, headed by Martin Seligman, which also happens to offer the first master's degree in Positive Psychology (MAPP). Seligman is one of the field's founders. His book *Authentic Happiness: Using the New Positive Psychology to Realize Your Potential for Lasting Fulfillment* covers the field's basic principles.

Others, like Barbara Fredrickson at the University of North Carolina at Chapel Hill, study positive emotion in psychophysiology laboratories.

When one tries to find research on "joy" it is nearly impossible to isolate researchers who deal solely with the concept of joy. As suggested above, most fields of study related to joy are dedicated to positive psychology or happiness research. I recommend the following books and websites as places to start if one is seriously interested in the field.

Websites

World Database of Happiness (Extensive happiness research resource). http://www.worlddatabaseofhappiness.eur.nl/hap_bib/bib_fp.htm

Ed Diener, PhD, psychologist and researcher on Subjective Well-Being, Department of Psychology, University of Illinois at Urbana-Champaign. http://s.psych.uiuc.edu/~ediener/

Barbara Fredrickson, PhD, director of the Positive Emotion and Psychophysiology Lab, University of North Carolina, Chapel Hill. http://fredrickson.socialpsychology.org/

National Center for Complementary and Alternative Medicine, National Institutes of Health. http://nccam.nih.gov/health/meditation

The Psychoneuroimmunology Research Society. http://www.pnirs.org/

The Association for the Advancement of Applied Psychoneuroimmunology. http://www.lifecoachusa.com/aaapni/

Laughter Yoga Movement. http://www.laughteryoga.org/

Dr. Michael Miller's research at the University of Maryland
http://www.umm.edu/news/releases/laughter2.htm

Indiana State University, Psychoneuroimmunology Theory Information.
http://www.indstate.edu/mary/pnipage.htm

Author's website: www.jephostetler.com

Bibliography

Augsburger, David. *Caring Enough to Forgive: True Forgiveness.*
Scottdale, Pa.: Herald Press, 1981.

Berk, L. S., S. A. Tan, et al. "Neuroendocrine and stress hormone
changes during mirthful laughter," in *American Journal of
Medical Sciences*, 1989 Dec:298(6):390-6.

Cousins, Norman. *Head First: The Biology of Hope and the Healing
Power of the Human Spirit.* New York: E. P. Dutton, 1989.

———. *Anatomy of an Illness as Perceived by the Patient.*
New York: Norton, 1979.

Groopman, Jerome. *The Anatomy of Hope: How People Prevail in
the Face of Illness.* New York: Random House, 2004.

Hageseth III, Christian. *A Laughing Place: The Art and Psychology
of Positive Humor in Love and Adversity.* Fort Collins, Colo.:
Berwick Publishing Company, 1991.

Hostetler, Jeptha R. "Humor, Spirituality and Well-being," in *Perspectives on Science and Christian Faith*, Volume 54, Number 2, June 2002.

Klein, Allen. *The Healing Power of Humor: Techniques for Getting Through Loss, Setbacks, Upsets, Disappointments, Difficulties, Trials, Tribulations, and All that Not-So-Funny Stuff.* Los Angeles: Tarcher/Putnam, 1989.

Pearsall, Paul. *Super Joy: Learning to Celebrate Everyday Life.* New York: Doubleday, 1988.

Seligman, Martin. *Authentic Happiness: Using the New Positive Psychology to Realize Your Potential for Lasting Fulfillment.* New York: Free Press, 2002.

Stepanek, Jennifer Smith, ed. *Reflections of a Peacemaker: A portrait through Heartsongs.* Alexandria, Va.: VSP Books, 2005.

Stepanek, Mattie J. T. *Heartsongs.* Alexandria, Va.: VSP Books, 2001.

———. *Journey through Heartsongs.* Alexandria, Va.: VSP Books, 2001.

———. *Celebrate through Heartsongs.* New York: Hyperion, 2002.

———. *Hope through Heartsongs.* New York: Hyperion, 2002.

Appendix B

The Marathon Bible Verses

These verses were handwritten from memory by my mother, Luella Hostetler, age ninety-one. She confided that since she had memorized these verses when she was nine years old, in 1919, some of the words were not correct or in the correct order. They are presented here as she wrote them. She acknowledged that the letter X is not quite right and that the letter Z may be from the middle of a verse.

She sent this list of verses about a week before I ran my fourth Columbus marathon. She had no idea that a marathon is twenty-six-plus miles (which is very handy for a twenty-six-letter alphabet).

A — And be ye kindhearted, tender and forgiving to one another, even as Christ has loved and forgiven you.

B — Believe on the Lord Jesus Christ and you shall be saved.

C — Create in me a clean heart oh God, and renew a right spirit within me.

D — Delight thyself also in the Lord and he will give you the desires of thine heart.

E — Even a child is known by his doings, whether they are pure and right.

F — Fear God and keep his commandments.

G—Go ye into all the world, preaching the gospel, teaching them to observe all things I have commanded you, and I will be with you always.

H—Honor thy father and mother that the days may be long upon the earth.

I —I am the way the truth and the life. No man cometh unto the father but by me.

J —Jesus said, "Suffer the little children to come unto me, for of such is the kingdom of heaven."

K—Keep thy tongue from evil and thy lips from speaking guile.

L —Lying lips are an abomination to the Lord and those who deal truly are His delight.

M—My sheep hear my voice and know me, and follow me.

N—Now is the accepted time, and now is the day of salvation.

O—Open my eyes that I might see the beauty of holiness.

P —Peace I give unto you, not as the world gives, give I my peace to you.

Q—Quench not the spirit.

R —Remember the Sabbath day to keep it holy.

S —Search the scriptures, for in them you seek eternal life and in them you know you have eternal life.

T—Thy Word is a lamp unto my feet and a light unto my pathway.

U—Unto you is born this day, in the city of David, a Savior that is Christ the Lord.

V —Verily, verily I say unto you, this is the Savior born unto you.

W—Whether ye eat or whether ye drink, do it unto the Lord.

X—Except a man be born again, he cannot enter into the kingdom of heaven.

Y—Ye are the light of the world; a city that is set on a hill cannot be hid.

Z—Zion city shall come down from the heavens.

Appendix C

The Joy Card

This card is public domain and, as such, you are free to copy it, change the words, and use it as you see fit. The only caveat is that you keep the black and light squares where they are and give credit to having heard about it from this book.

HOPE	HEALTH	PLAY	JEST
LAUGHTER	LOVE	FESTIVITY	JOY
MIRTH	SMILES	FOOD	FUN

1. Place finger on any BLACK square.
2. Slide your finger **right** or **left** to the nearest LIGHT square. (May have to go over a dark square to get to a light one.)
3. Slide your finger straight **up** or **down** to the nearest DARK square. (May have to go over a light square to get to a dark one.)
4. Move **diagonally up** or **diagonally down** to the nearest LIGHT square.
5. Finally, move **left** or **right** to the nearest DARK square. (May have to go over a light square or two to get to the dark one.)

You will always end up on the **JOY** square.

Appendix D

From a Towel to a Chicken

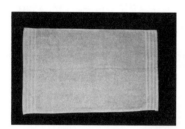

Fig. 1—Hand towel.

Fig. 2—Roll up one end.

Fig. 3—Roll up other side as well.

Fig. 4—Fold ends over.

Fig. 5—Pull out tips.

Fig. 6—Four tips out.

Fig. 7—Rotate bundle ¼ turn.

Fig. 8—Pull two top and two bottom tips, unrolling towel.

Fig. 9—Chicken body.

Fig. 10—Allow bottom legs to spring apart.

The Author

Jep Hostetler has spoken about joy for nearly twenty years. He has inspired audiences throughout the United States, India, Nepal, China, and Europe. Magical entertainment is always a part of Jep's presentations. He is a member of and has served as international president of the International Brotherhood of Magicians. Jep and his wife, Joyce Metzler Hostetler, are graduates of Goshen College. Jep holds a doctorate in human anatomy from The Ohio State University College of Medicine and has researched connections between humor and well-being. He lives in Columbus, Ohio, and is active in the Columbus Mennonite Church. He is the author of numerous articles about health, spirituality, and humor.